PRESENTED TO:

....

FROM:

....

DATE:

....

10

MINUTES

IN THE WORD

John

10 *Minutes in the Word: John*
Copyright © 2019 by Zondervan

Requests for information should be addressed to:

3900 Sparks Dr. SE, Grand Rapids, Michigan 49546

ISBN 978-0-310-45192-1

Cover art direction: Kathy Mitchell

Interior design: Kristy Edwards

Printed in China

19 20 21 22 23 24 25/ DSC / 6 5 4 3 2 1

Contents

Introduction

John's gospel is among the most loved and well-known books in the Bible. Author and theologian D. A. Carson said of the fourth gospel, "John is simple enough for a child to read and complex enough to tax the mental powers of the greatest minds."[1] John's gospel differs from the other three gospels in a variety of ways. Matthew, Mark, and Luke are known as the Synoptic Gospels. The word *synoptic* derives from a Greek word that means "to see together."[2] Although the Synoptics each convey their own specific themes, the three books share much in common, such as their sequences and common wording, and are similar in the way they present the time line of Christ's life and ministry. On the other hand, more than 90 percent of the material contained in John's gospel is not found in the Synoptics.

Christians, seekers, and skeptics have been turning to John's gospel for almost two thousand years to read about the life and ministry of Jesus Christ. John, also known as the "fourth evangelist" and "the beloved disciple," was forthcoming about his motivation for writing. Near the end of his gospel, he wrote, "But these are written that you may believe that Jesus is the Messiah, the Son of God, and that by believing you may have life in his name" (20:31).

The Word Became Flesh

In the beginning was the Word, and the Word was with God, and the Word was God. He was with God in the beginning. Through him all things were made; without him nothing was made that has been made. In him was life, and that life was the light of all mankind. The light shines in the darkness, and the darkness has not overcome it.

—*John 1:1-5*

J ohn's gospel is both simple and profound. It has been compared to a pool that is shallow enough that a child can wade in and deep enough for an elephant to swim in. Some of the most profound themes are found in the opening verses, known as the prologue (John 1:1–18). John's gospel is about the Word. But what does he mean by the "Word"? In the Old Testament, God's Word refers to His mighty self-expression in creation, revelation, and salvation. The personification of the Word makes it appropriate for John to apply it as a title to God's own Son, Jesus Christ, who is the ultimate expression of God's self-disclosure.[3]

In his opening verses, John took great care to declare the supremacy of Christ (vv. 1–5). Jesus Christ, the Word, God's divine choice of self-expression, existed in the beginning, so one might rightly assume that the Word was either with God or was God Himself. John asserted the Word was both. There has never been a time when the Word didn't exist. Christ created all things in the history of the universe, and all things depend on Him for existence. The supremacy of Christ is a theme that the apostle Paul echoed when writing about Jesus: "For in him all things were created: things in heaven and on earth, visible and invisible, whether thrones or powers or rulers or authorities; all things have been created through him and for him. He is before all things, and in him all things hold together" (Colossians 1:16–17).

John declared Jesus to be "the light [that] shines in the darkness" (John 1:5). In John's gospel, the contrast between light and darkness is a consistent theme that runs throughout the entire book. Light and darkness are not merely opposites; darkness is a synonym for evil. Those who are apart from the light of Christ, the incarnate Word, prefer darkness because of their evil behavior. When the light exposes their deeds, they recoil because they don't want to be exposed. John made it clear that light and darkness are not equals, but that light always prevails: "The light shines in the darkness, and the darkness has not overcome it" (v. 5). Still, we can anticipate that people will reject the light (vv. 10–13).

Father, help me see the supremacy of Christ in all things. Teach me to live in a way that reflects the truth that I was created by Jesus and for Jesus. Help me rest in the fact that in Christ all things hold together. I ask that my study of John's gospel will deepen my understanding of the person and work of Jesus Christ and that I will love Him more.

Are you mindful of the fact that you were created by Jesus and for Jesus? How does this truth impact your daily living? Practically speaking, how does Jesus hold things in your life together? When was the last time you saw evidence of His grace?

The Testimony of John the Baptist

John replied in the words of Isaiah the prophet, "I am the voice of one calling in the wilderness, 'Make straight the way for the Lord.'"
—*John 1:23*

Read John 1:19-28

W e live in an era and culture where it's common to draw attention to ourselves. Whether it's garnering attention on social media, making a reputation for ourselves in the workplace, or pursuing an elevated societal status, self-promotion is considered the norm. When John the Baptist began his ministry, he was drawing crowds and becoming well-known. The gospel of Matthew says, "People went out to him from Jerusalem and all Judea and the whole region of the Jordan" (3:5). It's not surprising that the Jewish authorities were curious about a new preacher gaining a large following, so they sent priests and Levites from Jerusalem to ask him some questions.

In first-century Palestine, speculation about the identity of the coming Messiah was rampant, so it's easy to see why the authorities began by asking John about his identity. Upon questioning, John immediately denied that he was the Christ. He also denied that he was Elijah or a prophet. When they pressed him to elaborate on his identity, he didn't boast about the crowds he was drawing or the recent success of his ministry. Instead, "John replied in the words of Isaiah the prophet, 'I am the voice of one calling in the wilderness, "Make straight the way for the Lord"'" (John 1:23).

It's refreshing to see that John the Baptist's response didn't even contain a hint of self-promotion. Unlike so many people in today's culture who intentionally attempt to inflate their self-worth, John made it clear that he was subordinate to Jesus. His reason for coming was not to win a popularity contest, but rather to make a name for Jesus. He had a deep understanding of his purpose, which was to point others to the Messiah. John went out of his way to avoid making a name for himself. In God's kingdom, this is the path to greatness. Jesus described John the Baptist this way: "Truly I tell you, among those born of women there has not risen anyone greater than John the Baptist; yet whoever is least in the kingdom of heaven is greater than he" (Matthew 11:11).

Our purpose in this life is not unlike that of John the Baptist. As Christ-followers, we are not here to make a name for ourselves. We are here to point people to Jesus. Modern-day culture might insist that the way up is to draw attention to oneself, but the Bible teaches another way: "For those who exalt themselves will be humbled, and those who humble themselves will be exalted" (23:12).

Father, forgive me for all the ways I am prone to self-absorption. Help me be quick to repent when I seek glory for myself. Empower me to live in a way that points other people to Jesus.

In what areas are you prone to self-promotion? Are you tempted to draw attention to yourself? Why is self-promotion a recipe for misery? How can you use your life to point people to Jesus?

Jesus Calls the First Disciples

The next day John was there again with two of his disciples. When he saw Jesus passing by, he said, "Look, the Lamb of God!" When the two disciples heard him say this, they followed Jesus. Turning around, Jesus saw them following and asked, "What do you want?" They said, "Rabbi" (which means "Teacher"), "where are you staying?" "Come," he replied, "and you will see."

—John 1:35–39

F ew, if any, topics have been more controversial than the identity of Christ. Some people believe Jesus was a wise teacher and a rabbi. Others think He was a prophet and a martyr. And some, of course, believe Him to be the long-awaited Messiah promised throughout the Old Testament. When John the Baptist encountered Jesus, he said, "Look, the Lamb of God!" (John 1:36). Two of John the Baptist's disciples overheard his declaration and followed Jesus.

When Jesus saw the two men following Him, He initiated a conversation with them by asking, "What do you want?" (v. 37). This is a question we must all answer. Potential Christ-followers must count the cost of discipleship. In Luke's gospel, Jesus warned a potential disciple who pledged to follow Him that as a disciple he may find himself homeless: "Jesus replied, 'Foxes have dens and birds have nests, but the Son of Man has no place to lay his head'" (Luke 9:58). Jesus never indicated that following Him would be easy. In fact, He promised the opposite (John 15:18–25). But Christ-followers experience a relationship with Jesus that far outweighs potential risks.

The two men asked Jesus where He was staying. "Come," He replied, "and you will see" (John 1:39). As a result, the men went to where Jesus was staying and spent the rest of the day with Him. In the first century, disciples literally followed a teacher and learned from the words and actions of their mentor. The fact that the men asked Jesus where He was staying indicated their intention of becoming His disciples. Jesus doesn't call His followers to a life of dry religion; He invites us to a vibrant relationship with Him. As modern-day believers, we follow Christ by studying and obeying His Word, cultivating an intimate prayer life, and being an active worshipper in a local church.

....

Father, I pray You will give me a heart that loves Jesus above all things. I ask that I will want nothing more than I want Him. Lead me into a deeper relationship with Him as I study Your Word. Grant me a willingness to follow Him regardless of the cost.

....

What do you want in life? Are you as close to Christ as you'd like to be? Do you sense Jesus inviting you to enter into a deeper relationship with Him? Are you willing to follow Christ into hardship? What evidence have you seen that makes following Jesus worth the risk?

The Wedding at Cana

What Jesus did here in Cana of Galilee was the first
of the signs through which he revealed his glory; and
his disciples believed in him.

—*John 2:11*

In John 2, we find Jesus, along with His mother and disciples, attending a wedding in Cana. In the ancient world, weddings were major social events, and it wasn't uncommon for the celebration to last up to a week. Unlike today, when it's customary for the bride's parents to pay for the wedding, it was the groom's responsibility to finance the wedding expenses. In the Middle East, hospitality was, and still is, taken seriously. Running out of wine would've resulted in terrible embarrassment and might've caused the new couple and their families to be labeled with a social stigma for the rest of their lives.[4]

Mary's concern for the situation suggests she might have been involved in overseeing the wedding celebration. She anxiously told Jesus, "They have no more wine" (v. 3). Jesus' polite but abrupt response signaled a transition in their relationship (v. 4). The term *woman* was considered a polite but not intimate form of address, much like using *ma'am* in our modern-day culture. Jesus' public ministry was about to begin, and His earthly relationships would not dictate His actions. Instead, He was acting according to the Father's timetable. Mary was unfazed and told the servants, "Do whatever he tells you" (v. 5).

Jesus told the servants to fill the six stone jars sitting nearby with water. These were large containers with a capacity to hold 20 to 30 gallons each. By making such a large amount of wine (120 to 180 gallons), not only would He meet the needs of the celebration and spare the couple social embarrassment, but the leftover wine was an extravagant gift for the new couple.

Jesus' first recorded miracle was not simply a powerful demonstration of compassion but was intended to reveal Jesus' identity. When John told of Christ's miracles, he referred to them as "signs." The Greek word for "sign" is *semeion*, which refers to a sign that distinguishes a person or thing from others.[5] By using this term, John was indicating that Jesus didn't perform miracles for their own sake, but with the intention of pointing the observers to Himself.

....

Father, thank You that You are a God who has
revealed Yourself through the person and work
of Jesus Christ. Help me have an ever-increasing
understanding of Christ's identity and His power.
Thank You that You are a compassionate God.
Empower me to extend Your compassion to
others.

....

**Are you mindful that Jesus faithfully reveals
His identity to you through His Word and His
power? How do Jesus' acts of compassion
impact your view of Him? How have you
experienced His compassion in your own life?**

Jesus Cleanses the Temple

His disciples remembered that it is written: "Zeal for your house will consume me."
—*John 2:17*

Read John 2:13–22

A t some point, there's a good chance you've visited a heavily populated tourist district. Whether it's an amusement park, a national landmark, a museum, or a popular area in a city, big crowds often drive up prices. A few times each year, the city of Jerusalem has always been known to swell with people who come to observe the religious feasts. Jesus traveled to Jerusalem to observe both the Passover and the Feast of Unleavened Bread, which immediately followed. The Feast of Passover is celebrated to observe Israel's deliverance from slavery in Egypt and to remember when the Lord struck down the firstborn of the Egyptians but passed over the homes of the Israelites (Exodus 12:23–30). Passover is celebrated annually on the fourteenth day of Nisan, which lands in March or April.[6]

When Jesus arrived, He undoubtedly found Jerusalem booming with Jewish pilgrims who had traveled from all over the Roman world to celebrate. Passover brought big business to local business owners. Since it was impractical for travelers to transport animals to sacrifice at the feast, local merchants set up shop in the temple complex and sold the animals required for the sacrifice at massively inflated prices. Also, every Jewish male older than twenty had to pay the yearly temple tax, and it had to be paid by using

Jewish or Tyrian coins (30:13–14). The money changers exchanged their money for acceptable currency but charged outrageous fees to do so. What had started as a service to the worshippers had become exploitation of the people of God.

Jesus was outraged at what He saw. The impurity of what was transpiring in the temple was dishonoring to God, and Jesus took action by driving all the merchants out of the temple with a whip. Undoubtedly there was chaos in the temple court. Jesus' actions were entirely appropriate, and His response reminds us of His deity and His messiahship. Jesus is the loyal Son of God and will not permit the Father's house to be dishonored. Jesus' intention that day was to purge the temple of impure worship. God's people are to approach worship with reverence.

Father, thank You for the gift of being able to enter Your church as a house of worship. Lord, be quick to rebuke me when I am irreverent. Teach me to prepare my heart for worship and to worship You with all I have and with all I am.

What do Jesus' actions tell us about the importance of worship? How satisfied are you with the degree of worship in your own life? What steps can you take to approach worship with reverence?

You Must Be Born Again

Jesus replied, "Very truly I tell you, no one can see the kingdom of God unless they are born again."

—*John 3:3*

A ll of us need a handful of people who are willing to speak truth into our lives. A well-timed conversation with someone we respect has the potential to change our course. In John 3, Jesus spoke life-changing truth to Nicodemus. Nicodemus was a prominent man among the religious ranks of Israel. He was a Pharisee and a member of the Sanhedrin, the ruling body of the Jewish people. Nicodemus's prominent standing as a member of the Sanhedrin likely explains why he came to see Jesus at night. It's probable that he didn't want his visit to be interpreted as the Sanhedrin's stamp of approval on Jesus' ministry, and he also didn't want to risk the disapproval of other members for talking with Jesus.[7]

When Nicodemus spoke to Jesus, he called Him "Rabbi" (John 3:2), which is a title of respect signaling that Nicodemus was addressing Jesus as an equal. Many of Nicodemus's contemporaries were suspicious and hostile toward Jesus, but nothing in Nicodemus's behavior suggested the same. Nicodemus conceded that he believed God was with Jesus based on the miracles He was performing (v. 2). But Jesus had no desire to discuss miracles. Instead, He cut to the heart of the matter and told Nicodemus that no one would see the kingdom of God unless they were born again (v. 3). Jesus was communicating the life-transforming nature of genuine saving faith. Regeneration, or the new birth, is an act of God by which He imparts eternal life to those who were previously dead in sin (Ephesians 2:1).

Understandably, Nicodemus had some questions. Jesus' words must've been staggering for a man who had spent his entire life observing the law and the rituals of Judaism. Nicodemus was a man of rank among the religious men of Israel, and Jesus was telling him that human effort had no power to save. Although nothing in this account suggests that Nicodemus became a Christ-follower that night, later Nicodemus boldly defended Jesus before the Sanhedrin (John 7:50–51), and he helped Joseph of Arimathea prepare Christ's body for burial (19:38–39). Both of these actions indicate Nicodemus may have taken Jesus' words to heart and that he came to understand and experience the new birth.

Father, thank You for Your plan of salvation. Thank You that because of Christ we can experience a new birth and enter Your kingdom. Help me rely solely on Christ and His finished work on the cross for my salvation.

> **Do you find it hard to accept that salvation is not based on works but is attained by grace through faith in Christ? What merits are you prone to rely on rather than grace? How has the gospel confronted you with the reality that you need to put your faith in Christ rather than yourself?**

Jesus and the Woman of Samaria

Jesus declared, "I, the one speaking to you—I am he."

—*John 4:26*

I t's been said that you can tell a lot about a person by the company he or she keeps. In John 4, we find Jesus having a theological discussion with an immoral woman from Samaria. It would've been unthinkable for an ordinary Jewish man to speak with a woman, a Samaritan, or an immoral person in public. But Jesus wasn't ordinary, and He demonstrated a pattern of seeking out the least likely people to engage.

There had been a long history of tension between the Jews and Samaritans, and as a rule, Jews went out of their way to avoid passing through Samaria. But Jesus intentionally traveled through Samaria on His way to Galilee. On this day He was sitting near a water well at high noon as He waited for His disciples, who had gone into town to get food. As He waited, a woman approached the well, and Jesus asked her for a drink. Ordinarily, women traveled in groups in the early-morning hours to retrieve water. The fact that this woman was alone and coming to the well at the hottest time of the day indicates that she was an outcast in her own community. For obvious reasons, she was shocked when Jesus spoke to her.

Soon a theological conversation unfolded, and Jesus introduced the topic of living water, and He informed the woman that those who partake of the living water will never again thirst (v. 14).

The woman asked Jesus for this living water, and Jesus changed the subject to her personal life. The woman's history suggests she was looking for peace and fulfillment in romantic relationships and things had turned out poorly. Jesus pressed the issue, which forced her to acknowledge her sin history as He addressed the fact that she'd had five husbands and was now living with a man. Quickly, the woman concluded that Jesus' knowledge of her past came from God, and she thought He was a prophet. After a brief discussion about principles of worship, the conversation turned to Jesus' identity. The woman mentioned she understood that the Messiah was coming (v. 25), and then Jesus informed her, "I, the one speaking to you—I am he" (v. 26).

Jesus could've revealed His identity in a public announcement to Roman dignitaries, politicians, or the most notable men of the first-century culture. Instead, He chose a minority woman who was an outcast in her own community. Jesus revealed her sin problem and then provided the remedy. He does the same for us today. Regardless of our past, Jesus invites us to partake of the living water that is found only in Him.

Father, I thank You that regardless of the sins in my past, Jesus invites me to partake of the living water. Give me the strength I need to repent and turn from my sins, and I pray my deepest needs and longings will be met in Christ.

What sins do you need to acknowledge to Christ? Have you experienced the living water that satisfies your deepest needs and longings?

Jesus Heals an Official's Son

Then the father realized that this was the exact time at which Jesus had said to him, "Your son will live." So he and his whole household believed.

—*John 4:53*

N one of us enjoy feeling desperate, but spiritually speaking, there are times when desperation is a gift. Jesus had created a stir in Cana when He turned the water to wine, and when He returned there, word had gotten around, and a royal official was waiting for Jesus, with the hope He could heal his critically ill son. Most parents will go to any length to get treatment for a sick child, and this man was no exception. The royal official was a man with status and wealth, but despite his financial resources and connections, his son remained deathly ill, and the man was desperate.

When the royal official approached Jesus, his belief in Christ was not yet based on a desire for salvation and eternal life but rather was driven by desperation for his son's illness, and he begged Jesus to go home with him to his son. Jesus refused and issued a rebuke: "'Unless you people see signs and wonders,' Jesus told him, 'you will never believe'" (John 4:48). And then, instead of agreeing to travel to Capernaum with the official, Jesus instantly healed his son. At this point, the man had no confirmation that the boy had recovered, but he took Jesus at His word and departed. As he traveled home, he learned that his son had been healed at the exact time Jesus had said he was. The man knew Jesus had performed a miracle and spared his son's life. The text indicates that the mighty demonstration of Jesus' power moved the nobleman from sign-seeking unbelief to genuine saving faith that impacted the entire household (v. 53).

Experiencing turmoil is never fun, and most of us would prefer to avoid it. But times of stress and turmoil have the potential to open our eyes to spiritual truths we wouldn't see if all were well. The royal official had come to the end of his resources when he'd tried everything to help his sick son, and nothing had worked. In desperation, he turned to Jesus. Not only was his son healed, but he and his entire household experienced saving faith in Christ. Desperation has the ability to drive us to the arms of Christ, and when it does, we should consider it a gift.

Father, I pray that I will experience Jesus in such a way that I seek Him and not merely the things He provides for me. Let my shortcomings be blessings that drive me closer to Christ and deepen my faith.

Do you seek Christ, or only what He can do for you? Have you experienced a time when desperation has driven you closer to Jesus?

The Healing at the Pool on the Sabbath

In his defense Jesus said to them, "My Father is always at work to this very day, and I too am working."
—*John 5:17*

If you've wrestled with a problem for a long time, it's tempting to believe things will never improve. When Jesus met a man at the pool at Bethesda, he had been suffering from paralysis for thirty-eight years. Jesus asked him, "Do you want to get well?" (John 5:6). Sadly, the man failed to understand Jesus' proposal. Instead of responding with a resounding "Yes!" the man told Jesus all the reasons he'd not been healed. Like many people who have struggled with a chronic problem, the man's expectations of what Jesus could do for him were reduced to what he believed was possible.[8] Jesus ignored the man's history of defeat and said, "Get up! Pick up your mat and walk" (v. 8). Instantly, the man was healed.

In most cases, a healing of this magnitude would be a reason for celebration. But Jesus performed the healing on the Sabbath, and the Jewish leaders were furious (v. 16). Jesus' refusal to obey legalistic, man-made laws was an ongoing point of contention between Jesus and Israel's religious leaders. Undoubtedly, Jesus wanted to show mercy to this man and heal him, but the man's condition wasn't life-threatening, and his healing could've been performed any day of the week. Jesus wanted to both heal him and point out that Israel's religious leaders were guilty of substituting their man-made traditions for God's commands (Matthew 15:9).[9]

To be sure, the Old Testament prohibited working on the Sabbath, and the Israelites were not to labor as they did during their weekly employment. But rabbinic tradition added thirty-nine additional expectations to the list of activities they were to avoid. One of those activities included carrying a mat or pallet, and therefore the religious leaders accused the man who had been healed of breaking the law. They cared more about their legalistic laws than they did about a paralysis victim who had suffered for thirty-eight years. Jesus not only cured the man's paralysis, but He called attention to the problem in the religious leaders' hearts.

Jesus is filled with compassion, and during His earthly ministry He routinely healed people and alleviated their suffering. In a twinkling of an eye, Christ can bring a problem to an end that we've wrestled with for decades. But He also cares about our character. Christ-followers are called to care about other people and place the needs of others over man-made expectations.

Father, thank You for being filled with compassion for those who suffer. Help me remember that You have the power to change my circumstances even when I can't see how You will.

Is there an area in your life you've struggled with for years? Do you believe Jesus can fix the situation even if you can't see how?

Jesus Feeds Five Thousand

Jesus then took the loaves, gave thanks, and distributed to those who were seated as much as they wanted. He did the same with the fish.
—*John 6:11*

Read John 6:1–15

L arge crowds of people were following Jesus as He traveled across the region, preaching the Word of God and healing the sick. The masses weren't following Him because they'd decided to serve Him as Lord. Instead, they were following Him because of the miracles He had performed (John 6:2). As Jesus sat down with His disciples, He surveyed the crowd. Although the text says there were five thousand men there, counting the women and children, there were easily two to three times that number in attendance. Jesus asked Philip, "Where shall we buy bread for these people to eat?" (v. 5), even though they were a long way from anywhere a meal could be purchased. Jesus already knew the answer but asked for Philip's benefit. Jesus had already performed numerous miracles, but His disciples didn't understand what Jesus was about to do.

Jesus saw there was a lack of food before anyone requested a meal or voiced a complaint. He'd anticipated the needs of the people. Traveling on foot for a long distance had likely depleted the energy of the crowd. Undoubtedly, many were following Jesus because they were sick and hoped to be healed. Walking all day without proper nutrition would've proven dangerous for the medically vulnerable. It's notable that Jesus didn't blame the crowd for poor planning and leave them to the consequences of their lack of food. He simply said, "Have the people sit down" (v. 10). He also didn't instruct them to pace the mountainside, worrying about where their next meal would come from. Instead, by telling them to sit down, He put them in a posture to receive.

The text says Jesus took a little boy's five small barley loaves and two small fish, gave thanks, and distributed food to the crowd until they were full. Obviously, if Jesus had the power to heal the sick, He possessed the ability to provide miraculously. Jesus didn't just provide barely enough; He offered so much that there were leftovers. Keep in mind that the majority of the crowd were not Christ-followers but were merely following Jesus because they were curious or wanted something from Him. Jesus is aware of our needs before we are and has ways of meeting our needs that we could never anticipate. A failure or mistake on our part doesn't mean He won't take care of us. Jesus is a God of compassion and provides for us in ways that we can't provide for ourselves.

....

Thank You, Lord, that You are filled with compassion for Your people. Help me trust You in my areas of need. I pray that I will be mindful that before I am even aware of my problems, You have a solution.

....

Do you need Christ's provision in a specific area? What does this passage tell you about His willingness and ability to provide?

"I Am the Bread of Life"

Then Jesus declared, "I am the bread of life. Whoever comes to me will never go hungry, and whoever believes in me will never be thirsty."
—*John 6:35*

Read John 6:22-59

I n the Gospels, when Jesus says the words, "Truly, truly" or "Very truly," it means that He is getting ready to communicate an important truth that He wants His audience to give their full attention to. When a crowd of seekers found Jesus in Capernaum and inquired about when He had arrived, Jesus responded, "Very truly I tell you, you are looking for me, not because you saw the signs I performed but because you ate the loaves and had your fill" (John 6:26).

Jesus was calling attention to the reality that the crowds were seeking Him for what they could get from the miracles He performed, and they were missing the spiritual significance of His identity and mission. Unlike Christ's disciples, the masses were seeking the gifts rather than the Giver. Jesus rebuked them for their selfish materialism and encouraged them to be mindful of their spiritual need (v. 27). They misinterpreted Jesus' words and believed He was communicating that they needed to do some works to merit eternal life (v. 28). But salvation cannot be obtained by works. It is a gift from God that comes by grace through faith in Christ (Ephesians 2:8–9; Acts 4:12). Our material needs are short-lived and are often of little consequence, while our spiritual needs bring ramifications that will impact us for eternity.

Jesus did not come to earth as a mere miracle worker. Jesus is the Son of God and the promised Messiah. His miracles served to authenticate His message, but the miracles were not sufficient for salvation. Jesus said, "Very truly I tell you, the one who believes [in me] has eternal life. I am the bread of life" (John 6:47–48). Jesus is the sustenance for every need we will face in this life. His provision far exceeds the material blessings that too often preoccupy our thoughts. Jesus came to address our sin problem and provide a way to experience eternal life by being reconciled to the Father (14:6).

Father, I pray that I will be mindful of my spiritual needs. Forgive me for the times I've sought You for only what You could do for me. Give me a heart that seeks the Giver rather than the gift.

Are you prone to seek Jesus for material provision while ignoring your spiritual needs? Do you seek the gift more than you seek the Giver? In this season of life, what is your greatest need?

The Words of Eternal Life

Simon Peter answered him, "Lord, to whom shall we go? You have the words of eternal life. We have come to believe and to know that you are the Holy One of God."

—*John 6:68-69*

A careful reader of the Scriptures will occasionally come across what theologians refer to as "hard sayings." This term refers to things that are hard for us to understand or seem harsh. In John 6, Jesus said some things that caused some of His audience to leave His company. On numerous occasions in John's gospel, we see fickle seekers who are curious about Jesus' miracles but never become true disciples of Christ. In this case, however, those who walked away from Jesus had previously identified themselves as disciples but proved not to be when they abandoned Him. Jesus was left with the original twelve, and one of those Jesus referred to as a "devil" (v. 70).[10]

Jesus watched as His false disciples walked away and rejected the only God who could save them. Despite the difficult teaching, Christ did not apologize for His words, nor did He alter them to suit His listeners' preferences. Jesus asked the remaining disciples, "You do not want to leave too, do you?" (v. 67). Peter didn't deny that Jesus' teaching was difficult, but he acknowledged that Jesus spoke the words of eternal life (v. 68). Peter said, "Lord, to whom shall we go?" (v. 68).

Scores of people today identify themselves as Christ-followers until they read something in the Scriptures that they disagree with or is difficult to accept. Rather than praying through the texts of Scripture they don't understand and studying until they have clarity, they abandon the faith. Others quit following Jesus because they are uncomfortable with a controversial teaching. As Christ-followers, we are called to obey and accept the whole counsel of God, even the parts that make us uneasy. Like Peter, we don't have to deny that some teachings are difficult. But genuine Christ-followers don't choose to obey and adhere to the teachings we are comfortable with while disregarding the rest.

Father, I pray that You will give me increased insight into the areas of Scripture that I have a hard time understanding. Lord, even when the teaching is difficult, I pray I will have a heart and mind that obeys You because I know You hold the words of eternal life.

What portions of Scripture make you uncomfortable? Have you prayed and asked God to give you increased clarity? Have you studied these passages in depth? Will you continue to follow Christ even when you find teachings that are difficult to accept?

Can This Be the Christ?

Then Jesus, still teaching in the temple courts, cried out, "Yes, you know me, and you know where I am from. I am not here on my own authority, but he who sent me is true. You do not know him, but I know him because I am from him and he sent me."

—John 7:28–29

Read John 7:25–31

Despite Jesus' preaching, signs, and miraculous healings, there continued to be division in regard to His identity, and many people were plagued with unbelief. The Feast of Tabernacles was about to take place in Jerusalem, and Jesus' brothers pressed Him to make a grand entry and announce His identity (John 7:3–5). But Jesus refused and chose to arrive quietly when the festival was half-way through, and then He went straight to the temple courts and began to teach (vv. 14–15). Predictably, His presence caused a commotion, and the Jewish leaders were so hostile toward Jesus they sought to have Him arrested (v. 32). The crowd's response to Jesus varied: some attempted to inflict violence on Him, while others believed He was the Messiah (vv. 30–31).[11]

As Jesus spoke, some of the Pharisees were so driven to silence Him they attempted to seize Him (v. 30). Israel's religious leaders didn't even want their citizens to speculate about Jesus, and some people were openly insinuating He was the Messiah. The Pharisees were so alarmed by Jesus' influence that they partnered with the Sadducees, a religious group they differed from theologically, to join forces in their hatred against Jesus. Despite their attempts to silence Jesus, they were unable to lay a hand on Him because "his hour had not yet come" (v. 30). Jesus was operating according to

His Father's time frame. Not even a hostile mob could kill Jesus before the appointed hour, because He had come to fulfill His Father's will, and nothing could thwart His mission. Men wouldn't choose the time of Christ's death; it was determined by the Father.

Father, thank You that Jesus is who He says He is. Help me understand that His lordship covers every aspect of my life. There are no areas that are beyond Jesus' control. Teach me to trust Him in every situation and circumstance.

Despite having ample reason to believe Jesus was the Messiah, many people continued in unbelief. In what areas of life are you prone to struggle with unbelief? Do you believe Jesus is the Messiah but wrestle with whether He is able or willing to meet specific needs in your life? If Jesus is indeed who He says He is, what then is beyond His capability? In what areas do you need to trust His lordship?

The Woman Caught in Adultery

"Then neither do I condemn you," Jesus declared. "Go now and leave your life of sin."
—*John 8:11*

J esus was in the temple courts, teaching the Word of God, when the scribes and Pharisees brought Him a woman who had been caught in the act of adultery. The religious leaders made an example out of her and forced her to stand in front of the group to impose the highest degree of embarrassment. Adultery was a serious violation of the Old Testament law, and it called for a severe penalty or even death by stoning. The Law of Moses read, "If a man is found sleeping with another man's wife, both the man who slept with her and the woman must die. You must purge the evil from Israel" (Deuteronomy 22:22). But the man involved in this adulterous act was curiously absent, and the woman was left to face the shame and penalty alone.

In reality, the scribes and Pharisees had no desire to uphold the law of adultery, and they weren't motivated to clean up the moral climate of Jerusalem. Instead, they were publicly humiliating this woman with the goal of trapping Jesus. They hoped they could corner Jesus and prompt Him to say something contrary to the law "in order to have a basis for accusing him" (John 8:6). But Jesus didn't fall for their scheme.

As they spoke their allegations against the woman, Jesus bent over and began to write on the ground with His finger. The text is silent about what Jesus wrote, but there have been numerous speculations. One plausible possibility is that Jesus was writing things the accusers themselves were guilty of. Although we can't be certain what Jesus wrote, He said, "Let any one of you who is without sin be the first to throw a stone at her" (v. 7). Jesus was pointing out that they were hypocritically merciless to a fellow human being who had sinned. Although these were highly educated religious men, practically speaking they had no concept of the grace of God.

One by one her accusers departed, and she was left standing with only Jesus. When Jesus asked, she told Him none had condemned her. "'Then neither do I condemn you,' Jesus declared. 'Go now and leave your life of sin'" (v. 11). Simply put, Jesus instructed her to be done with that way of living. As a forgiven woman, it was time for her to leave her sinful lifestyle and walk in newness of life.

Father, thank You for the grace You have lavished on me by sending Christ as the substitute for my sins. I pray grace will be my first response when other people sin.

Do you find it difficult to extend grace to those who have sinned? In what areas of your life has Jesus shown mercy to you? How have His mercy and grace changed your heart and the way you respond to others who stumble?

The Truth Will Set You Free

"If you hold to my teaching, you are really my disciples. Then you will know the truth, and the truth will set you free."

—*John 8:31–32*

A ll human beings seek truth, because none of us want to live our lives based on lies.

Modern-day culture is quick to teach that there are multiple versions of truth and many paths to God. Of course, that is incorrect. The Bible plainly teaches there is only one path to God, and that is through Jesus Christ (John 14:6; Acts 4:12). Jesus was speaking to a group of Jews who believed He was the Messiah when He said, "If you hold to my teaching, you are really my disciples. Then you will know the truth, and the truth will set you free" (John 8:31–32).

Jesus made a distinction between those who were His disciples and those who weren't. In John 6, some of Christ's disciples abandoned Jesus, proving that they didn't possess genuine saving faith. They believed for a short while and then fell away. Jesus said His true disciples hold to His teaching, and as a result, know the truth, and the truth sets them free.

It's not uncommon for someone to make a profession of faith in Christ but then lose interest. Jesus said the litmus test for a true disciple is whether he or she holds to His teaching. As we study God's Word, we are subjected to truth, and the Scriptures shape our hearts, minds, and character. As we abide in Christ, we come to know Him, our love for Him grows, and our desire to obey Him increases with each passing day. As the love of Christ overwhelms our hearts, sin loses its allure and becomes something we genuinely want to avoid.

Father, thank You that You have made it possible for all people to know and live in Your truth. Lord, empower me to abide in Christ and know Him in such a way that I love Him more with each passing day. Help me hold to His teaching and make it evident that I am His disciple.

Practically speaking, how do you seek truth in your own life? As you study the Scriptures, how does God reveal the truth to you? As your knowledge of God's Word grows, do you hold to Christ's teaching? Would you describe yourself as a disciple of Jesus?

Children of the Heavenly Father

Jesus said to them, "If God were your Father, you would love me, for I have come here from God. I have not come on my own; God sent me."
—*John 8:42*

Read John 8:39–47

There's an old cliché that says, "The apple doesn't fall from the tree." The point of the saying is that children often act like their parents. Jesus was having a heated conversation with a group of Jews who claimed they were children of Abraham, and He boldly pointed out that they weren't acting like Abraham. In fact, they were looking for a way they could kill Jesus, and their behavior was demonstrating the characteristics of the devil (John 8:44).

Jesus described Satan as both a liar and a murderer. Satan ushered in the spiritual ruin of the human race when he lied to Eve in the garden of Eden by telling her, "You will not certainly die" (Genesis 3:4). Satan is a master deceiver, and his tactics are subtle. The Enemy routinely makes it his business to delude people and prevent them from seeing the glory of God (2 Corinthians 4:4). By rejecting Jesus, the Jewish leaders were unwittingly identifying themselves as children of the Enemy. Since the father of lies deceived them, they were not able to accept the truth. As a result, Jesus said, "Whoever belongs to God hears what God says. The reason you do not hear is that you do not belong to God" (John 8:47).

The only way out of Satan's web of deception is through the truth that is found in Christ. Jesus said, "So if the Son sets you free, you will be free indeed" (v. 36). Jesus' teaching destroyed the notion that there is hope or security found in being Abraham's descendants or in any other identity. Thankfully, those who are under the influence of the Enemy have the opportunity to repent and place their faith in Jesus. The hope of eternal life is found only in the finished work of Jesus Christ, and those who believe prove themselves to be children of their Father in heaven (v. 47).

Father, thank You that You have permitted me to know the truth that is found in Your Son, Jesus Christ. I ask that You will help me be quick to discern truth from lies. I pray that I will abide in Your Word so that I know the truth and will be able to spot the lies of the Enemy.

Are you mindful of the fact that the Enemy attempts to deceive you with doubt, fear, and lies? Which are you most prone to succumb to? What role does God's Word have in fighting the Enemy's deception with the truth? Do you regularly pray that God will keep you free from Satan's destructive strategies?

Jesus Heals a Man Born Blind

"Neither this man nor his parents sinned," said Jesus, "but this happened so that the works of God might be displayed in him."

—*John 9:3*

When we experience a season of suffering, it's tempting to believe that we have done something wrong and that God is disciplining us, but that's not always the case. Jesus was traveling with His disciples when the group saw a man who had been blind since birth. The disciples suspected that the man's blindness was caused by sin, so they asked Jesus, "Rabbi, who sinned, this man or his parents, that he was born blind?" (John 9:2). But Jesus corrected their misguided thinking and told them the man's blindness was not a result of anyone's sin, but rather so that the works of God might be displayed in him (v. 3).

It is true that sin does at times cause suffering and affliction (Numbers 12:1–10; 2 Samuel 12:15–23), but there are other times when people experience suffering due to no fault of their own. In the book of Job, Job's friends were convinced that some action on Job's part must have caused the devastating chain of events he endured. But we know that Job's afflictions were no fault of his own.

Jesus told His disciples the reason the man had been born blind was so the works of God might be displayed in his life, and that's precisely what happened. Jesus healed him, and for the first time in his life, he could see (John 9:7). Jesus not only healed this man's physical blindness, but He also cured his spiritual blindness. The

Pharisees were once again livid that Jesus had healed on the Sabbath, and they threw the healed man out of the synagogue (v. 34). When Jesus heard what had transpired, He found the man and initiated a conversation about his faith. Jesus revealed His identity, and the man responded, "Lord, I believe," and worshipped Him (v. 38).

There are times it's difficult to know the reason for our suffering, and there will be times we may never know why. But for those who love God, suffering is never in vain. The apostle Paul wrote, "And we know that in all things God works for the good of those who love him, who have been called according to his purpose" (Romans 8:28).

Father, I thank You that for those of us who love You, our suffering is never wasted. I pray that You will bring good from the circumstances that are causing me pain. When I sin, help me be quick to repent and experience restoration. When my suffering comes because of other reasons, give me the faith to trust You.

Do you believe God can work even suffering for your good? In what situation do you need to trust Jesus to bring good in the midst of affliction?

"I Am the Good Shepherd"

"I am the good shepherd. The good shepherd lays down his life for the sheep."
—*John 10:11*

The Scriptures refer to Jesus by numerous titles, but one of the most prevalent in John's gospel is that of Shepherd. Hundreds of years before the Messiah came, the Old Testament predicted He would shepherd His people (Ezekiel 34:23). In John 10, Jesus used the metaphor to describe Himself and how He relates to the sheep. Jesus said, "I am the good shepherd. The good shepherd lays down his life for the sheep" (v. 11). At the time, Jesus' audience didn't realize He would lay down His life for His followers at Calvary.

Shepherding was a profession that everyone in Israel's culture was familiar with because it was part of everyday life. It was common knowledge that sheep are helpless, prone to wander, defenseless, and dirty animals.[12] Sheep require constant supervision, leading, and redirection, or they will not survive. Tending sheep has proven to be practical training for leading people. The Patriarchs—Abraham, Isaac, and Jacob—all spent time as shepherds. But not all shepherds in Israel were good ones. Some were harsh and abusive or cared nothing for the sheep. Jesus represented a different type of shepherd.

In the ancient Near East, it was common for a shepherd to walk ahead of his flock, making sure the area was safe and that predators wouldn't threaten the sheep. Sheep follow their shepherd because they recognize his voice and refuse to respond to others with whom they are unfamiliar. In the same way, Christians become familiar with Jesus' voice and can discern it from all others. Jesus is faithful to His flock, constantly guiding, leading, and redirecting His people on the path He intends. Genuine believers in Jesus Christ recognize "His voice" in the truth of God's Word and reject anything that is not in alignment with the Scriptures. True Christ-followers will never abandon Jesus to follow a false shepherd, but will trust Christ with their lives.

Father, I pray that You will give me the ability to discern Jesus' voice from all others. I ask that You will help me be able to detect things in my life that don't line up with the truth of Your Word. I pray that I will listen for Jesus' voice more than any other.

Do you recognize Christ's voice in the midst of all the other things competing for your attention? What role does Scripture play in discerning God's will for your life? Are you able to differentiate things in the world that do not line up with the truths of God's Word?

The Death of Lazarus

So when he heard that Lazarus was sick, he stayed where he was two more days, and then he said to his disciples, "Let us go back to Judea."
—*John 11:6–7*

Read John 11:1-16

I f you are a Christian, there's a good chance you've questioned God's timing. It's often been said God's timing is perfect: He is never early, and He is never late. In the opening verses of John 11, Jesus received word that His dear friend Lazarus was sick. Mary, Martha, and Lazarus were three grown siblings who lived in Bethany, and Jesus was close with the entire family and loved them deeply.

Oddly, Jesus did not immediately travel to Lazarus's bedside when He received the news that his friend was ill. Instead, He lingered and said, "This sickness will not end in death. No, it is for God's glory so that God's Son may be glorified through it" (v. 4). Two days later, Jesus told His disciples that it was time for them to travel to Judea, and they reminded Jesus that the last time they were there the Jews tried to stone Him to death (v. 8). But Jesus was unfazed and was adamant they return: "So then he told them plainly, 'Lazarus is dead, and for your sake I am glad I was not there, so that you may believe. But let us go to him'" (v. 15).

Jesus made this statement because He knew what He would do, and He knew His disciples, as well as Lazarus's family, would see the glory of God manifested in a way that would profoundly influence their faith. But for now, Jesus' disciples, as well as Lazarus's loved ones, were left wondering why Jesus had tarried. After all, if Jesus had arrived on time, He could've healed Lazarus and prevented his death. From their vantage point, it looked as if Jesus had failed them and disregarded their suffering.

All Christ-followers will experience times when it seems as if God is disengaged from our problems. We'll be left to wait, and we won't understand why. But the Scriptures teach us time and again that Jesus is fully engaged and acquainted with His people's circumstances. When we can't see God working, we shouldn't assume He isn't. God works in ways we are unaware of.

Father, I pray that You will replace my fear with faith. When I am tempted not to trust Your plan and provision, I pray that I will be quick to remember Your promises and remind myself of all the ways You have worked on my behalf in the past.

Do you find it hard to trust God when you can't see or sense Him working in the midst of your hardships? Do you find yourself questioning God's goodness when you don't have all the answers? Practically speaking, how do these passages speak to your uncertainty?

"I Am the Resurrection and the Life"

> Jesus said to her, "I am the resurrection and the life. The one who believes in me will live, even though they die; and whoever lives by believing in me will never die. Do you believe this?"
>
> —*John 11:25–26*

. . . .

W hen Jesus arrived in Bethany, Lazarus had already been buried four days. Understandably, his sisters were distraught, and when Martha heard Jesus was on the way, she went out to meet Him. "'Lord,' Martha said to Jesus, 'if you had been here, my brother would not have died. But I know that even now God will give you whatever you ask'" (John 11:21–22). Martha demonstrated a tremendous amount of faith in this statement. Her relationship with Jesus was close enough that she felt comfortable being completely transparent.

Jesus simply said, "Your brother will rise again" (v. 23). Martha wasn't sure if Jesus was referring to the resurrection at the last day or if He was planning on raising Lazarus from the dead. But then Jesus said something profound: "I am the resurrection and the life. The one who believes in me will live, even though they die; and whoever lives by believing in me will never die. Do you believe this?" (vv. 25–26). In other words, Jesus was saying He didn't just *teach* the resurrection; He *is* the resurrection, and He has power of life, death, and the grave.[13] In response to Jesus' question, "Do you believe this?" Martha replied with one of the greatest confessions of faith in all of Scripture. "'Yes, Lord,' she replied, 'I believe that you are the Messiah, the Son of God, who is come to the world'" (v. 27).

In the grips of sorrow, Martha made a statement that demonstrated her faith and that she had inherited eternal life.

Undoubtedly, Martha didn't understand why the events had unfolded the way they did. Surely she was devastated with grief. But her emotions and lack of understanding didn't diminish her faith in Christ. She knew Jesus was who He claimed to be, and she knew He would do as He promised.

Father, I pray that my relationship with Christ will be so close that I can ask the hardest of questions. I ask that even in the midst of grief, my faith in Him will be confident.

> **Like Martha, can you approach Jesus with total transparency and ask Him difficult questions? Do you know Him well enough to trust Him even when you don't understand why things happen the way they do?**

Jesus Weeps

When Jesus saw her weeping, and the Jews who had come along with her also weeping, he was deeply moved in spirit and troubled. "Where have you laid him?" he asked.

—*John 11:33-34*

Read John 11:28-37

....

When someone dies, it can be difficult to know what to say to a grieving loved one. As a result, sometimes people unintentionally say things that aren't helpful. Those who have experienced periods of grief will often relate that the most meaningful gestures of sympathy contained no words; the well-wisher's willingness to be present in the midst of their loss served as the greatest comfort of all.

When Jesus arrived in Judea, Mary and Martha were grieving the death of their brother, Lazarus. When Jesus saw Mary and the Jews who had accompanied her weeping, He was deeply moved and asked, "Where have you laid him?" (John 11:34). On the way to the tomb, Jesus wept. Jesus' tears were likely a result of His love for Lazarus and His hatred for the effects of sin in this world.[14] The act of Jesus' weeping is a beautiful demonstration of His humanity. The Old Testament describes Jesus as "a man of suffering, and familiar with pain" (Isaiah 53:3). The Jews speculated that Jesus loved Lazarus, and that was an accurate assessment. But others questioned Jesus' ability to heal Lazarus, and they wrongly thought Jesus' tears were void of hope. Jesus was on the verge of carrying out His greatest miracle yet, and still He took time to grieve with His friends.

The Bible teaches Christ-followers to be present with our friends and loved ones during times of grief and celebration. The apostle Paul wrote, "Rejoice with those who rejoice; mourn with those who mourn" (Romans 12:15). We don't need to have the perfect words of sympathy or try to explain things. Just being present with those who are suffering is an act of kindness that has the most potential to help.

Father, thank You for creating all human beings with emotions. I am grateful Jesus is willing to enter into our greatest areas of suffering. Teach me to be helpful to those who are grieving, and I pray I will be ready to be present not only in times of celebration but also in times of mourning.

> **Do you struggle with showing your emotions in times of grief? Have you ever wondered how you should respond to someone who is grieving? What does Jesus' willingness to weep communicate to you about the value of tears?**

Jesus Raises Lazarus

Then Jesus said, "Did I not tell you that if you believe, you will see the glory of God?"
—*John 11:40*

W hen Jesus approached Lazarus's tomb, He was deeply moved and asked for the stone to be removed (John 11:38–39). Martha didn't understand that Jesus intended to raise Lazarus from the dead, and she was concerned that her brother's body had begun to decompose after four days in the tomb. It wasn't Jewish practice to embalm, but instead, they used spices to mask odorous decay. After four days, Martha knew the spices would've been of little use. It's likely Martha assumed Jesus wanted to see Lazarus one last time, and she didn't want her brother to be viewed publicly in that state.[15]

Jesus said to Martha, "Did I not tell you that if you believe, you will see the glory of God?" (v. 40). Jesus was challenging Martha to shift her focus off Lazarus and onto Him. They did as Jesus asked and removed the stone, and Jesus began to pray. Jesus didn't ask the Father to raise Lazarus but thanked Him that He had heard His prayer (v. 41). After Jesus finished praying, He said in a loud voice, "Lazarus, come out!" (v. 43).

Jesus never used dramatic showmanship when He performed a miracle. His divine power was evident, and there was no need for theatrics. After the miracle, Jesus instructed the onlookers to unbind Lazarus from his graveclothes and let him go. It's notable that Jesus wasn't so taken with His own power that He overlooked the practical needs of the person.[16] Just as Jesus had told Martha she would, she and Mary, along with all the onlookers, witnessed the glory of God. In this miracle, Jesus demonstrated that He holds power over death, and there is nothing outside of His sovereignty.

Father, I praise and worship You, for You are even more powerful than death. There is nothing outside of Your control, and nothing is too hard for You. Lord, I ask that You will increase my faith and give me opportunities to see Your glory.

Do you have a hard time believing that God can bring about the impossible? Like Martha, do you tend to place your focus on the problem rather than on Christ? How does Lazarus's story speak to you in regard to God's timing?

Mary Anoints Jesus at Bethany

Then Mary took about a pint of pure nard, an expensive perfume; she poured it on Jesus' feet and wiped his feet with her hair. And the house was filled with the fragrance of the perfume.

—*John 12:3*

Read John 12:1-8

T here's an old saying that goes, "Listen to what they say, but believe what they do." The point is, it's easy to talk a good talk, but people will ultimately act on what they believe to be true. That was the case for Mary. After Jesus raised Lazarus from the dead, Mary and Martha invited Jesus back to their home and hosted a dinner in His honor. During the meal, Mary took a pint of pure nard, which was a costly perfume, and poured it on Jesus' feet. The perfume was worth about one year's salary for the average worker, and Mary used it all in a matter of seconds.[17]

It was an extravagant act of love and devotion, and Mary wasn't conservative in demonstrating her adoration for Jesus. Then, in an act that shocked everyone at the table, Mary dried Jesus' feet with her hair. In Jewish culture, washing another's feet was considered degrading labor and was only done by a slave, and to be washing His feet with her hair was an even greater act of submission. Mary was undeterred by the cost of the perfume or the threat to her reputation. She was motivated to express her love for Jesus.

Judas Iscariot was at the meal and disapproved of Mary's extravagant gesture. Judas attempted to protest by advocating for the poor, but John revealed what really motivated Judas's disdain. Judas preferred the money stay in the treasury because he had been pilfering from the money bag (John 12:6). Jesus defended Mary's act of devotion. "'Leave her alone,' Jesus replied. 'It was intended that she should save this perfume for the day of my burial. You will always have the poor among you, but you will not always have me'" (vv. 7–8). Jesus wasn't saying the poor should be ignored. He was pointing out that He would only be with them for a short time and they would have their whole lives to serve the poor.

Father, I pray that I will treasure Jesus in such a way that I will offer my best worship. I ask that You give me a heart that loves Him the way Mary did. I pray that I will worship Jesus sacrificially. Help me be mindful that Jesus didn't give His minimum to me at Calvary. I pray that I won't give minimally to Him.

Does your worship for Jesus accurately demonstrate how you feel about Him? Do you give Christ your best offering or do you give minimally? Why was Mary motivated to show her love for Jesus? What motivates you to reveal your love for Him?

The Plot to Kill Lazarus

So the chief priests made plans to kill Lazarus as well, for on account of him many of the Jews were going over to Jesus and believing in him.

—*John 12:10-11*

Read John 12:9–11

I f you keep up with current events in global Christianity, you know that Christians around the world routinely suffer for their allegiance to Christ. In the West, few have been called to suffering or martyrdom, but the reality is it's always a possibility in the Christian faith. Jesus told His disciples, "You will be hated by everyone because of me, but the one who stands firm to the end will be saved" (Matthew 10:22).

Mary, Martha, and Lazarus had hosted a dinner to honor Jesus. Many from the large crowd of Jews who were in Jerusalem to observe the Passover heard that Jesus was in Bethany, and they traveled there to see Him. The news about Lazarus being raised from the dead had spread, and people were talking. The crowd wanted to see not only the miracle worker but also the man whom Jesus had raised from the dead.

The curious crowd wasn't openly hostile to Jesus in the same way that the religious leaders were, but they also weren't committed followers. As the people flocked to Bethany to see Jesus and Lazarus, they caught the attention of the Jewish religious leaders. The chief priest was already planning to kill Jesus (John 11:53), and now the leaders planned to murder Lazarus as well. Lazarus was living proof of Jesus' divine power and messianic claims.[18] As a result, Lazarus posed a threat to the religious leaders because many were coming to faith in Christ because of his testimony.

No one takes a neutral stand when it comes to Jesus Christ. There are some, like Mary and Martha, who are committed followers. Others are merely thrill seekers. And some people, like the Jewish religious leaders, are so opposed to Christ that they hate Him. Those leaders loathed Him with such a vengeance they plotted His death.

Father, I pray that my faith would be so rooted in Christ that people would readily identify me as a Christ-follower. I pray that if the time ever comes for me to suffer because of my faith, Your Holy Spirit will give me the strength to endure whatever opposition is necessary.

How would you describe your stance on Christ? Are you, like Lazarus, Mary, and Martha, close enough to Jesus that others would associate you with Him?

The Son of Man Must Be Lifted Up

"Now my soul is troubled, and what shall I say? 'Father, save me from this hour'? No, it was for this very reason I came to this hour. Father, glorify your name!"

—*John 12:27–28*

A s Jesus' earthly ministry pulsed forward, the cross drew near. Jesus knew His death was the foundation of God's redemptive plan, but Jesus didn't approach Calvary with detachment or indifference. Jesus experienced intense dread because He understood He would bear the shame of the world's sin, experience the Father's wrath, and for a time, be separated from His Father's presence. The text describes Jesus' soul as being "troubled" (John 12:27). The Greek word means literally "to shake" or "to stir up." It denotes the intense mental and spiritual agitation of being upset or unsettled.[19]

As Jesus spoke, He asked a hypothetical question: "Now my soul is troubled, and what shall I say? 'Father, save me from this hour'?" (v. 27). Jesus was unwilling to deviate from God's plan of redemption, and He immediately answered His own question: "No, it was for this very reason I came to this hour" (v. 27). Then, for the third time in Jesus' earthly ministry, the Father's voice was heard from heaven: "I have glorified it, and will glorify it again" (v. 28).

Jesus told the crowd that the Father's voice was for their benefit (v. 30). On previous occasions, when Jesus was baptized and at the transfiguration, the Father's voice audibly communicated that He was pleased with His Son (Matthew 3:17; 17:5). Now, as the cross loomed, the Father authenticated Jesus' mission and assured the disciples that His imminent death was not a sign of disapproval. In fact, just as He had glorified His name through Jesus' life and ministry, He would again glorify it in His death. Jesus said, "And I, when I am lifted up from the earth, will draw all people to myself" (John 12:32). Jesus shared this to indicate the type of death He would suffer, but the disciples failed to understand Him.

Father, I thank You for Your plan of redemption that is found in the finished work of Christ Jesus. I pray that as I read John's account of Christ's ministry, I will see and feel a measure of what Christ experienced on my behalf. I pray that I will live my life in awe of His sacrificial love and respond accordingly.

Those of us who have been Christ-followers for many years and have heard the story of the cross numerous times are at risk of becoming apathetic to the intensity of Christ's suffering. As you read John's account of the time leading up to the cross, what new insights do you see? How would you describe His mission of glorifying the Father? How does Christ's suffering impact you?

Jesus Washes the Disciples' Feet

"Now that I, your Lord and Teacher, have washed your feet, you also should wash one another's feet." —*John 13:14*

O ne of the ways pride manifests itself in modern-day culture
is the average person's aversion to menial tasks. We live in a
society that is prone to entitlement, and there is a false sentiment
that it's better to have servants than to serve others. But in one
simple act, Jesus set the standard for a different way of living.

Just before the Passover, Jesus gathered His disciples. He knew
the time of His earthly ministry was quickly coming to a close, and
He wanted to share a meal with them. As dinner progressed, Jesus
got up from the table and began to wash His disciples' feet (John
13:5). As we already saw with the story of Mary, in biblical times,
it wasn't even the proper protocol for a group of disciples to wash
a rabbi's feet. Foot washing was a task that was done by the lowest-
level slaves. The fact that Jesus had gotten up from the meal and
had undertaken the task of foot washing was unthinkable, and the
disciples were uncomfortable with the gesture. "'No,' said Peter,
'you shall never wash my feet.' Jesus answered, 'Unless I wash you,
you have no part with me'" (v. 8).

Judas Iscariot was likely among those who had his feet washed
by Jesus. Jesus knew that in just a matter of hours Judas would
betray Him, but Jesus still chose to serve him humbly (v. 10). Jesus
demonstrated that service to others shouldn't be contingent on

their behavior but should be motivated by love for God and people. After Jesus finished, He said to His disciples, "Now that I, your Lord and Teacher, have washed your feet, you also should wash one another's feet. I have set you an example that you should do as I have done for you" (vv. 14–15).

Jesus' command to humbly serve other people is counter-cultural to the times we are living in. Jesus' entire life and ministry destroy the notion that Christians are to be served. Instead, Christ-followers are to take on the role of a servant.

Father, I thank You for the perfect example of sacrificial living You have given me in the life of Christ. I pray that I will humble myself and serve others in the same manner Jesus did. I pray You will remove any shred of arrogance or self-entitlement from me and teach me that serving others is the way of gospel living.

Do you struggle with humbling yourself and taking on menial tasks? What does Jesus' willingness to wash the disciples' feet demonstrate to you about the role of serving others? Are you willing to extend kindness to someone you know would betray you? What does Jesus' gesture toward Judas teach about dealing with enemies?

A New Commandment

"A new command I give you: Love one another. As I have loved you, so you must love one another."
—*John 13:34*

F amily members often share specific characteristics simply
because they are related and have the same DNA. For instance,
it's not uncommon for children to look like one of their parents or
have similar traits that make it easy to identify them as a family
unit. Siblings may possess shared behaviors and tendencies because
they are raised in the same home and are heavily influenced by the
same people. A brother and sister share the same parents, genet-
ics, household rules, and atmosphere where they are raised. While
each child responds in his or her own way and develops a unique
personality, there are bound to be some shared similarities among
siblings.

As the time of Jesus' departure for the cross drew near, He spoke
with His disciples and warned that He would only be physically
present with them for a short time (John 13:33). Jesus knew His
time with His disciples was limited, and He most certainly used
the time He had left with them with intentionality. It was no time
for small talk. The conversations that Jesus had with His disciples
just before the cross were especially significant. Jesus told them,
"A new command I give you: Love one another. As I have loved
you, so you must love one another" (v. 34). Jesus even went as far
as to tell them that love would be the defining characteristic that

113

communicated to the world that they were His disciples. Jesus said, "By this everyone will know that you are my disciples, if you love one another" (v. 35).

It's notable that Jesus didn't tell His followers that they would be known for their ministries, knowledge, IQ, material possessions, bank accounts, personal appearance, political views, or accomplishments. He said those of us who follow Him would be identifiable by our love for one another. Jesus made it clear that for Christians, love should be the family trait that defines us. It is a sign of authenticity and indicates we belong to Him.

Father, I thank You for the love You have demonstrated to me by sending Christ to pay the penalty for my sins. I pray that I will be characterized by my love for all people and especially my brothers and sisters in Christ.

Is showing love to fellow Christians something that comes naturally to you, or is it difficult? Do you think most nonbelievers define Christians as people who love each other? What are tangible ways that you can demonstrate your love for your brothers and sisters in Christ?

"I Am the Way and the Truth and the Life"

Jesus answered, "I am the way and the truth and the life. No one comes to the Father except through me."

—*John 14:6*

A s mentioned in an earlier section, there's a good chance you've heard the saying, "There are many paths to God." It's a phrase that you've probably seen on T-shirts, on bumper stickers, and in self-help books, and it's a topic that's frequently discussed on talk shows. The problem is the statement isn't true.

As Jesus conversed with His disciples, He was preparing them for the events that were about to take place. Jesus had already told them He wouldn't be with them much longer, but they were unsure of where He was going (John 13:33; 14:5). Although it's obvious the disciples didn't understand what was about to transpire, they undoubtedly understood that things were about to change dramatically. These men had given up everything to follow Jesus, and Jesus wanted to prepare them for life after Calvary. Jesus said, "I am the way and the truth and the life. No one comes to the Father except through me" (John 14:6).

This is a staggering statement. Notice Jesus didn't say He was "a" way. He said He was "the" way. Then He drove home His point by adding, "No one comes to the Father except through me" (v. 6). In preparing His disciples for what was about to take place, Jesus wanted to be sure they understood there was no other route to salvation. In today's culture, this isn't a popular way of thinking.

Exclusive truth claims are often disregarded as narrow-minded. But this is the teaching we hear from the lips of Jesus, and it's repeated in multiple ways in the New Testament. The apostle Paul wrote, "Salvation is found in no one else, for there is no other name under heaven given to mankind by which we must be saved" (Acts 4:12).

As Christ-followers, we have to differentiate between common perceptions in mainstream culture and what the Bible teaches to be true. The Bible says Jesus is the only way to God: "Yet to all who did receive him, to those who believed in his name, he gave the right to become children of God" (John 1:12).

Father, I thank You that You have provided a way for me to be reconciled to You through the finished work of Christ. I am grateful for Your mercy and grace, and I pray I will live my life out of the overflow of Your love.

Do you believe that Jesus is the only way to be reconciled to the Father? How would you respond to someone who tried to convince you there are many paths to God? Why do you think people look for alternative options?

Jesus Promises the Holy Spirit

"I will not leave you as orphans; I will come to you."
—*John 14:18*

Read John 14:15–31

J ohn 14 falls in a section of Scripture that theologians refer to as the Farewell Discourse (John 14–17). This portion of Scripture has the longest section of teaching on the Holy Spirit found in the Scriptures. As Jesus spoke with His disciples, He assured them that although He would no longer be present with them in the physical sense, He would not abandon them. Jesus said, "I will ask the Father, and he will give you another Helper, to be with you forever" (John 14:16 ESV).

The Greek word John used for "helper" is *parakletos,* or in this context, *parakleton.*[20] It is the word from which we get the English word *paraclete.* The word is translated in numerous ways among Bible translations, including "advocate," "comforter," or "counselor." The term *advocate* provides insight into the role of the Holy Spirit. In ancient times, a paraclete was a defense attorney. If you were in trouble with the law and needed someone to represent you, a paraclete would be the person you would call. The word *para* is defined as "alongside" or "beside," and the verb *kletos* means "to call." So a paraclete is someone you would call to stand alongside you and represent you in your defense.

The term *comforter* is misleading. While it's true that the Holy Spirit does comfort us in our grief, the original rendering of this word denotes the idea "to strengthen." In the same way, the term *counselor* can misrepresent the role of the Holy Spirit. In our era, we often associate the term with a therapist or guidance counselor. But a *parakleton* was more readily defined as an advocate or counselor found in a courtroom who would defend you in front of a judge.[21]

Jesus didn't leave His original disciples as orphans, and He doesn't leave us to fend for ourselves. The Holy Spirit takes up residence in the life of every believer. The Holy Spirit has numerous roles, but one of the most crucial is to teach us truths about God. If we can comprehend spiritual truth, it's because the Holy Spirit has made it possible. The apostle Paul wrote, "The person without the Spirit does not accept the things that come from the Spirit of God but considers them foolishness, and cannot understand them because they are discerned only through the Spirit" (1 Corinthians 2:14).

Father, thank You for sending the Holy Spirit to live inside me. Through Him I will learn about You and deepen my spiritual life. Help me be sensitive to His words and attentive to how I respond to them.

> **Are you mindful of the Holy Spirit's work in your life? Do you rely on the third person of the Trinity in your day-to-day living?**

"I Am the True Vine"

"I am the true vine, and my Father is the gardener. He cuts off every branch in me that bears no fruit, while every branch that does bear fruit he prunes so that it will be even more fruitful. You are already clean because of the word I have spoken to you. Remain in me, as I also remain in you. No branch can bear fruit by itself; it must remain in the vine. Neither can you bear fruit unless you remain in me.

"I am the vine; you are the branches. If you remain in me and I in you, you will bear much fruit; apart from me you can do nothing."

—*John 15:1–5*

I f you've ever spent time with a child, there's a good chance you've heard the phrase, "I can do it on my own." Human beings are wired with a desire to be self-reliant. Of course, this is good to a point. We all want the children in our lives to grow up to be productive members of society who can care for themselves. But from a spiritual standpoint, the notion of self-reliance is both a delusion and a liability.

As Jesus spoke with His disciples just hours before going to the cross, He was preparing them for what was about to take place. For three years these men had walked shoulder to shoulder with Christ, learning what it meant to be His disciple, and they'd given up everything to follow Him. Jesus knew His disciples didn't understand what was looming at Calvary and that they'd be devastated by the coming events. Jesus loved these men, and He wanted them to thrive despite His physical absence. Interestingly, Jesus did not give them a pep talk or offer self-help advice. He didn't say, "I've taught you the ropes of Christian living and now I'm leaving it up to you to do your best."

Jesus was a master teacher, and in John 15 He used an agricultural illustration that everyone in that culture would understand. Jesus described Himself as the vine and His disciples as the branches. Anyone who knows about plant life understands that a branch is totally dependent on the vine for nourishment. A branch that is disconnected from the vine will quickly become malnourished and die. In the same way, Jesus instructed His followers to abide in Him in such a way that we draw our strength, power, and vitality from Him. He went as far as to say, "Apart from me you can do nothing" (v. 5). Notice He didn't say there are some things we can't do without Him. Instead, He said we can do nothing apart from Him. With those words, Jesus blew the notion of self-reliance to pieces. The Christian life is a call to a relationship with Jesus and a mindful dependence on Him for all things.

Father, Your Word makes it clear that I can do nothing apart from Christ. Help me understand that I am completely dependent on Your grace. Teach me to abide in Christ in such a way that I am empowered by His strength rather than my own.

Are you prone to self-reliance? In what areas of your life do you need to trust Christ for provision? How might your life be easier if you were to forsake self-reliance for faith in God's grace? Why is self-reliance a spiritual liability?

The Hatred of the World

"If you belonged to the world, it would love you as its own. As it is, you do not belong to the world. . . . That is why the world hates you."
—*John 15:19*

Read John 15:18–27

I n Christian circles, it's easy to spend so much time with our brothers and sisters in Christ that we are caught off guard when we are subjected to hatred from the world. In the safe cocoon of our Christian friendships, we are seldom, if ever, ostracized for our beliefs in Jesus. In the presence of our brothers and sisters in Christ, we are affirmed and embraced for our beliefs, and we should be. But Jesus warned His disciples to expect persecution from secular society.

Jesus said, "If the world hates you, keep in mind that it hated me first" (John 15:18). There is not a human being in the history of mankind who was subjected to more hatred than Jesus Christ. The prophet Isaiah wrote, "He was despised and rejected by mankind, a man of suffering, and familiar with pain. Like one from whom people hide their faces he was despised, and we held him in low esteem" (Isaiah 53:3).

Jesus came to a world that was hostile toward him, and yet He still willingly fulfilled His mission. Jesus came to do the will of His Father, and He was unconcerned with the personal cost. As Christ-followers, we can't expect all the blessings that come from belonging to God without being willing to suffer as a result of being associated with Him. Paul wrote, "Now if we are children, then we are heirs—heirs of God and co-heirs with Christ, if indeed we share in his sufferings in order that we may also share in his glory" (Romans 8:17).

As Christians, we shouldn't be surprised when the world rejects us because of our faith. But that unpleasant reality makes it that much more necessary for us to be actively involved in our local church so other Christians can support us. It's true that we will never avoid hatred from the world, and that's not the goal. But when we are confronted with hostility from the world, we will need our church family to encourage and support us.

Father, I pray that I will be mindful that Jesus endured an enormous amount of hate on my behalf. I pray that I will be willing to do the same for my faith and association with Him. Empower me to endure whatever persecution the world inflicts.

In what ways have you seen fellow Christians experience hatred from the world because of their faith? How can we encourage and support one another in times of adversity?

The Work of the Holy Spirit

"But when he, the Spirit of truth, comes, he will guide you into all the truth. He will not speak on his own; he will speak only what he hears, and he will tell you what is yet to come."

—*John 16:13*

....

A s the truth of Jesus' impending departure began to sink in, the disciples were filled with grief (John 16:6). In fact, the disciples were so consumed with their well-being they failed to show concern for what Jesus was about to endure. In actuality, they should have been comforting their Lord. But their thoughts were not focused on what the coming events would mean for Jesus, but only how they would be impacted.

Jesus pointed out that their grief was unwarranted. He said, "But very truly I tell you, it is for your good that I am going away. Unless I go away, the Advocate will not come to you; but if I go, I will send him to you" (v. 7). There was more than one reason why it was to their advantage that Jesus was "[going] away." The most obvious reason was that Christ going to the cross would provide atonement for their sins and provide a way for them and all people to be reconciled to the Father. But beyond salvation, if Jesus did not go away, the Holy Spirit would not come. Jesus had promised that the Holy Spirit would give them living water (7:37–39), reside in them (14:16–17), teach them (v. 26), empower their testimony, and activate the promises of God.[22]

Another role of the Holy Spirit is to convict the world of sin (John 16:8). Without an awareness of our sin problem, we will see no need for a Savior. The Holy Spirit's mission is to bring sinners to a saving knowledge of Jesus Christ. It's impossible for a man or woman to be saved apart from the Holy Spirit's convicting and regenerating work. Although the disciples were unable to see past their grief, Jesus was aware of the big picture and the ministry the presence of the Holy Spirit would usher in.

Father, I thank You that You love me enough to send the Holy Spirit to convict me of my sins. Teach me to be aware of His promptings, guidance, and conviction.

Why is being convicted of sin a positive thing and never a negative? What evidence of the Holy Spirit's work do you see in your own life? Do you live with a mindful presence of the Holy Spirit residing in you?

Your Sorrow Will Turn to Joy

"Very truly I tell you, you will weep and mourn while the world rejoices. You will grieve, but your grief will turn to joy."
—*John 16:20*

Read John 16:16–24

J esus spent His last evening before the cross comforting His disciples. Jesus understood that it's easier to endure a season of trial if there's an end in sight, so He spent time talking to His followers about the future. At this point, Jesus was just hours from the cross. Still, He reassured His disciples that the time of their suffering would come to an end and would be replaced with joy. In every sense, Jesus was preparing these men for what was about to transpire.

Although Jesus encouraged His disciples, He didn't sugarcoat what was about to happen. The disciples were about to enter a time of suffering. He told them they would weep and mourn and warned there would be others who would celebrate His death (John 16:20). Undoubtedly, the world's gloating would intensify their pain. However, Christ's enemies wouldn't celebrate for long. About the time the disciples' grief turned to joy, the world's celebration over Christ's death would turn to dismay.

Jesus compared what was coming to a woman giving birth. The pains of childbirth are agonizing but must be experienced. But after a woman gives birth to a child, she is so overjoyed with the baby that she quickly forgets the suffering caused by the labor (v. 21). In the same way, the disciples would experience intense grief, but when the reality of the risen Christ was manifested to them, their joy would be so intense their suffering would seem minimal. Jesus said, "So with you: Now is your time of grief, but I will see you again and you will rejoice, and no one will take away your joy" (v. 22).

For Christians, all suffering has an expiration date. No matter how dark our days may seem, the Bible teaches that all grief will come to an end and will be replaced with eternal peace and gladness. In the book of Revelation, the apostle John wrote, "'He will wipe every tear from their eyes. There will be no more death' or mourning or crying or pain, for the old order of things has passed away" (21:4).

Father, I thank You that because of Jesus a time is coming when all trials and suffering will come to an end. Until that day, empower me to persevere through my trials and anticipate the joy and peace that awaits all believers in Jesus Christ.

Do you anticipate the day when all suffering will come to an end? Do you look forward to the eternal joy and peace that will be experienced by all believers in Jesus Christ? How does knowing all suffering has an expiration date encourage you in this season?

The High Priestly Prayer

"Father, the hour has come. Glorify your Son, that your Son may glorify you."

—*John 17:1*

I n the High Priestly Prayer, Jesus prayed for Himself, His disciples, and His church. He began the prayer by saying, "Father, the hour has come" (John 17:1). On multiple occasions in John's gospel, Jesus spoke about His "hour." His hour referenced both His suffering on the cross and His exaltation because His glory would ultimately come from His suffering. The moment planned from the beginning had arrived, and Jesus went to the Father in prayer.

It's fascinating that even though Jesus was only hours away from excruciating pain and suffering, His thoughts had turned to the way He had spent His time on earth. He said, "I have brought you glory on earth by finishing the work you gave me to do" (v. 4). God's plan of redemption called for Christ coming to earth to save and seek the lost (Luke 19:10). Jesus brought glory to the Father during His time on earth by accomplishing the work He had given Him to do, and He knew He would be exalted to the right hand of the Father (Mark 16:19; Ephesians 1:20). With that in view, Jesus communicated His desire to return to the glory of heaven (John 17:5).

Jesus didn't limit His prayer to requests for Himself. Jesus prayed for His disciples and those who would become Christians in future generations. It's staggering to contemplate that just hours before the most monumental event in human history, Jesus prayed for His disciples, and He prayed for us. "My prayer is not for them alone. I pray also for those who will believe in me through their message" (v. 20). Jesus specifically prayed for His disciples: "Sanctify them by the truth; your word is truth" (v. 17).

Jesus understood that the human race was impacted by a distortion of the truth in the garden of Eden (Genesis 3). He knew the corruption that comes from false doctrine. So Jesus prayed that His disciples and all future believers would be sanctified by the truth that is found in God's Word. Christ-followers are called to be people of the Word, people of the truth.

Father, I thank You that You are the source of all truth, and I can know truth from lies if I am a student of Your Word. Thank You, Lord, for praying for me just hours before the cross. I pray that I will prioritize Your Word and prayer in my own life.

What role does God's Word play in your decision-making and day-to-day living? How does it impact you knowing Christ prayed for you just hours before going to the cross?

The Betrayal and Arrest of Jesus

Jesus commanded Peter, "Put your sword away!
Shall I not drink the cup the Father has given me?"
—*John 18:11*

J ohn's gospel doesn't provide us with the account of the agony Jesus experienced in Gethsemane. The other gospel accounts tell us Jesus was consumed with sorrow and asked for the Father to remove the cup that was before Him (see, for example, Matthew 26:38, 42). After Jesus prayed, He arose and crossed the Kidron Valley, and that is where John's account picks up (John 18:1).

Jesus' decision to go to the Kidron Valley was intentional. When travelers came to Jerusalem to celebrate the Passover, they were required to spend the night before the feast within the broader region of Jerusalem.[23] The Kidron Valley fell within this vicinity, and that's probably why Jesus chose this location. Judas, the disciple who would betray Jesus, also knew the spot because he had spent time with Jesus there as one of His disciples. Judas knew this was the likely location to find Jesus, and he led a group of soldiers there to seize Jesus (vv. 2–3).

As the men approached, Jesus asked, "Who is it you want?" (v. 4). Jesus didn't attempt to hide or fall into the shadows. Instead, He immediately revealed His identity. As soon as Jesus said, "I am he," the men drew back and fell to the ground (vv. 5–6). Again, Jesus asked who they were looking for, and He once again revealed His identity. Peter stepped forward to protect Jesus, and he cut off a man's ear (v. 10). But Jesus would not allow for resistance. "Jesus commanded Peter, 'Put your sword away! Shall I not drink the cup the Father has given me?'" (v. 11).

At any point, Jesus could have changed His mind. Certainly, He had the power to call the men off or do with them as He wished. But Jesus knew it was the will of the Father for Him to go to the cross, so He went without objection. He was arrested and bound and led off into the night by men who hated Him (vv. 12–13).

Father, I give You thanks and praise for Your plan of salvation. I thank You, Jesus, that You willingly went to the cross on my behalf. Help me obey You in all areas of my life.

How does knowing Jesus went willingly to the cross impact how you feel about Him? To what degree are you committed to doing the will of the Father? How would you describe your level of obedience to God?

The High Priest Questions Jesus

"I have spoken openly to the world," Jesus replied. "I always taught in synagogues or at the temple, where all the Jews come together. I said nothing in secret."
—*John 18:20*

J esus didn't get a fair trial. After His arrest, He was taken before a kangaroo court that had already made the decision to kill Him (John 11:53). Still, the Jewish authorities went through with a bogus hearing to give the impression that their decision was legitimate. Although they had no intention of adhering to the law or recognizing due process, they wanted to appear that they had.

In a legitimate legal proceeding, the authorities would've brought charges against Jesus and provided evidence to substantiate them. In Jesus' case, they had no real charges to bring against Him. So the high priest questioned Jesus about His teaching and His disciples with the goal of getting Jesus to say something incriminating. It was an illegal tactic that Jewish law forbade. Just as the Fifth Amendment of the United States Constitution protects the accused from having to testify against themselves, there were Jewish laws to guard against the same.[24] But in Jesus' hearing, the authorities didn't heed the laws.

However, Jesus was aware of the law. He answered, "I have spoken openly to the world. . . . I have always taught in synagogues or at the temple, where all the Jews come together. I said nothing in secret" (18:20). Jesus had nothing to hide. He had preached the gospel and offered salvation to the lost. He knew His accusers were not observing the law, so He asked them, "Why question me? Ask those who heard me. Surely they know what I said" (v. 21). Jesus' question shed light on their hypocrisy, and one of the officials responded by striking the Son of God in the face (v. 22). But Jesus did not retaliate. The apostle Peter wrote, "When they hurled their insults at him, he did not retaliate; when he suffered, he made no threats. Instead, he entrusted himself to him who judges justly" (1 Peter 2:23).

Father, I pray that when I am treated unfairly, I will remember that Jesus was too. I ask that You will help me respond like Jesus and be committed to doing Your will, despite the cost. I pray that regardless of how I am treated, I will respond in a way that honors You.

How do you respond when you are mistreated? Are you prone to retaliate? What does Jesus' response tell you about His character and His mission?

"My Kingdom Is Not of This World"

Jesus said, "My kingdom is not of this world. If it were, my servants would fight to prevent my arrest by the Jewish leaders. But now my kingdom is from another place."

—*John 18:36*

Read John 18:33-40

The Jewish leaders had been planning Jesus' death for some time (John 5:18; 7:1; 11:53). Until now, their plots had been thwarted because "his hour had not yet come" (7:30; 8:20). But now the hour had arrived, and with the help of Judas Iscariot, they arrested Jesus, and after a counterfeit trial, they sentenced Him to death. But they had no power to carry out the sentence because the Romans didn't grant them the authority to execute anyone, so they took Jesus before Pilate (18:30).[25]

By all accounts, it appeared Pilate wanted to avoid the situation. In fact, Pilate told those who had falsely incriminated Jesus, "Take him yourselves and judge him by your own law" (John 18:31). Pilate was fully aware that they wanted to kill Jesus, and the Jewish leaders admitted they didn't have the power to put Him to death (v. 31). This conversation fulfilled the word Jesus spoke about His death and the fact that Gentiles would be involved (Mark 10:33–34). When Pilate questioned Jesus, he asked, "Are you king of the Jews?" (John 18:33). In asking this question, Pilate was basically asking Jesus if He was pleading guilty or not guilty to the charges of insurrection. Jesus couldn't answer Pilate's question with a definitive yes or no without first defining what His kingship involved. "Jesus said, 'My kingdom is not of this world. If it were, my servants would fight to prevent my arrest by the Jewish leaders. But now my kingdom is from another place'" (v. 36).

After an extended dialogue, Pilate concluded that there was no basis to charge Jesus (v. 38). He offered the Jewish leaders a loophole. It was customary for one prisoner to be released at the time of Passover, and Pilate asked if they would prefer for Jesus to be released. The Jewish leaders and the crowd refused. Instead, they asked for Barabbas, a notorious murderer, to be released, and Jesus was sentenced to death by crucifixion (vv. 39–40; Matthew 27:16; Luke 23:19).

God, I offer praise and thanksgiving for the fact that Jesus endured unimaginable injustices and suffering on my behalf. When I am faced with hardships, teach me to rely on You in the same way Jesus relied on His Father.

Does knowing Jesus' history of suffering and injustice increase your faith that He understands your afflictions? How would you describe Jesus' demeanor as He faced injustices? How did His relationship with the Father impact His response? How does your relationship with Christ influence your behavior under stress?

Jesus Is Delivered to Be Crucified

Jesus answered, "You would have no power over me if it were not given to you from above. Therefore the one who handed me over to you is guilty of a greater sin."

—*John 19:11*

A desire for public approval is a temptation to avoid at any cost. A mob mentality had descended on Jesus' trial, and Pilate gave in to the pressure of the crowd. Pilate had declared he found no reason to charge Jesus, but then minutes later he turned Him over to be flogged (John 18:38; 19:1). Flogging was a horrendous form of punishment that called for the victim to be stripped and bound and repeatedly beaten by multiple men lined up to inflict torture with a crude instrument that tore apart the flesh. Jewish law limited the maximum number of blows to forty (Deuteronomy 25:3), but the Romans did not adhere to any restrictions.[26] The beating continued until the abusers were physically exhausted or the victim died. By the end of Jesus' flogging, His body had endured so much trauma He couldn't carry His cross to the execution site (Matthew 27:32).

The devastating blows to Jesus' body didn't satisfy His tormentors, so they mocked Him. They twisted a crown of thorns and put it on His head to add to His suffering and clothed Him in a purple robe to imitate the robes worn by royalty (John 19:2). They mockingly approached Jesus, saying, "'Hail, king of the Jews!' And they slapped him in the face" (v. 3). It's likely that Pilate had hoped they would release Jesus after His beating, but he underestimated their hatred for Jesus. Again, Pilate reiterated he found no basis to charge Jesus (v. 4). Pilate brought Jesus out to the crowd, but when they saw His bloodied and bruised body, they were not satisfied. "As soon as the chief priests and their officials saw him, they shouted 'Crucify! Crucify!'" (v. 6).

Pilate had grown increasingly uneasy and encouraged Jesus to speak for Himself. "Jesus answered, 'You would have no power over me if it were not given to you from above. Therefore the one who handed me over to you is guilty of a greater sin'" (v. 11). Jesus' point was that Pilate didn't have ultimate power over Him or the circumstances. It was the Father's will for Christ to go to the cross, and that's what kept Jesus from exerting His own power to save Himself (Isaiah 53:10). In the face of unspeakable suffering, Jesus trusted the Father's ultimate plan and coming victory.

Father, teach me to trust You even when I don't understand my circumstances. Empower me to obey Your will even before I know the outcome.

Do you find it difficult to trust God's will for your life? When you don't understand why things have gone in an undesirable direction, do you have faith that God is ultimately in control and will work out all things for the good for those who love Him?

The Crucifixion

Pilate had a notice prepared and fastened to the cross. It read: JESUS OF NAZARETH, THE KING OF THE JEWS.
—*John 19:19*

Read John 19:17–27

....

T he chain of events leading to the cross was unfolding just as the prophecies predicted they would. The unjust and counterfeit trial held by the Jewish leaders was over, and Jesus was sentenced to death by crucifixion. Jesus traveled to a place called Golgotha, and it was there soldiers nailed Him to a Roman cross, along with two other men, one on each side of Jesus (John 19:18–19). Although Jesus' suffering was unimaginable, John did not focus on the physical aspect of Christ's suffering but instead simply stated, "There they crucified him" (v. 18).

It was common practice for a criminal being led to his crucifixion to be accompanied by a sign that stated the crime for which he was being executed. Pilate took a last shot at the Jewish leaders and wrote, "JESUS OF NAZARETH, THE KING OF THE JEWS" (v. 19). To ensure everyone could read it, Pilate instructed that the inscription be written in Hebrew, Latin, and Greek, which were the three most commonly spoken languages in the region.[27] After Jesus was placed on the cross, the soldiers took His clothes and divided them among themselves. In doing so, they fulfilled the scripture: "They divide my clothes among them and cast lots for my garment" (Psalm 22:18).

Four women stood near the cross, and among them was Jesus' mother, Mary (John 19:25). "When Jesus saw his mother there, and the disciple whom he loved standing nearby, he said to her, 'Woman, here is your son,' and to the disciple, 'Here is your mother.' From that time on, this disciple took her into his home" (vv. 26–27). In Jesus' worst moments of suffering, He arranged for the apostle John to care for His mother. Even as Christ took on the sins of humanity, He was sacrificially tending to the practical needs of people He loved.

Jesus' crucifixion is the climax of redemption and God's plan for salvation. The cross of Christ is the most significant event in history. At the cross, God demonstrated the most supreme act of love while man simultaneously displayed sinful wickedness. Jesus could've come down from the cross at any moment, but He chose to stay. He stayed out of obedience to the Father and because of His love for us. "But God demonstrates his own love for us in this: While we were still sinners, Christ died for us" (Romans 5:8).

Father, I thank You for the gift of redemption, and I offer all praise and glory to Christ for His sacrifice on the cross. Teach me to love the way Jesus loved and to give my life sacrificially in service to others.

How has Jesus set the bar for us, His followers, concerning loving other people? How does the cross prove that our love for other people shouldn't be contingent on their behavior?

The Death of Jesus

When he had received the drink, Jesus said, "It is finished." With that, he bowed his head and gave up his spirit.

—*John 19:30*

C hrist's mission on the cross was near completion, but there was still one detail to be addressed. Even in the midst of His agony, Jesus, the omniscient Son of God, knew there was a remaining prophecy that had yet to be fulfilled, and so Jesus said, "I am thirsty" (John 19:28). King David had written, "They put gall in my food and gave me vinegar for my thirst" (Psalm 69:21). Jesus knew that communicating His thirst would prompt the soldiers to give Him a drink. The soldiers weren't acting in compassion. They intended to increase Jesus' suffering by prolonging His life. But in giving Jesus the sour drink, they unwittingly fulfilled the last remaining prophecy.

As soon as Jesus took the drink, He said, "'It is finished.' With that, he bowed his head and gave up his spirit" (John 19:30). Jesus didn't utter those words in defeat. He proclaimed victory. He had successfully atoned for the sins of the world and completed the mission the Father had given Him to do. The world didn't know it yet, but Satan had been rendered powerless, and death had been conquered (1 Corinthians 15:54–55; Colossians 2:15). Jesus had satisfied every requirement of God's righteous law, and every prophecy of Christ had been fulfilled.

Jesus' life wasn't taken from Him, but rather, He gave it up willingly. Jesus intentionally chose to surrender His life sacrificially. Earlier in John's gospel, Jesus had said, "No one takes it from me, but I lay it down of my own accord. I have authority to lay it down and authority to take it up again. This command I received from my Father" (John 10:18). Christ's death is the most meaningful event in human history. Although His disciples were devastated, they didn't yet understand the magnitude of what had transpired. That day at Calvary changed everything. Jesus didn't have to sacrifice His life, but He chose to. "And being found in appearance as a man, he humbled himself by becoming obedient to death—even death on a cross!" (Philippians 2:8).

Lord God, there is no way to adequately thank You for Christ's death on the cross that atoned for my sins. I ask, however, that my life will serve as a living expression of my love and gratitude for You. I praise You for Your plan of redemption.

How did God take the darkest day in human history and transform it into the most significant thing that ever happened to humanity? How does the cross demonstrate that things aren't always what they seem?

Jesus Is Buried

Because it was the Jewish day of Preparation and
since the tomb was nearby, they laid Jesus there.
—*John 19:42*

J esus' burial was different from that of most prisoners who were crucified by the Romans. When a Jew was executed, the family had the right to request the body, with the understanding the deceased couldn't be buried inside Jerusalem city limits. The Jewish authorities believed doing so would defile the sacred places, but the family could provide a proper burial in a different location.[28] But those who were crucified for sedition were typically left on the cross for several days, leaving them to the vultures as the ultimate insult. Jesus was spared this indignity. Perhaps out of feelings of guilt, or to get back at the Jews, Pilate agreed to release Jesus' body to Joseph of Arimathea and Nicodemus, even though they weren't immediate family (John 19:38–39).

Joseph of Arimathea was a wealthy man who possessed stature in the community and was likely a member of the Sanhedrin. He was a believer in Christ but had kept quiet about it. Earlier in his gospel, John had written, "Yet at the same time many even among the leaders believed in him. But because of the Pharisees they would not openly acknowledge their faith for fear they would be put out of the synagogue" (John 12:42). It appeared Joseph was among those in this group, but his faith motivated him to intervene to protect Jesus' body from additional indignity. Nicodemus, who had visited Jesus at night, was also a likely follower of Jesus (John 3) and brought supplies to prepare Jesus' body for burial.

In Jesus' death and burial, we begin to see a transition from the humiliation of the cross to Christ's exaltation in His death and burial. "He was assigned a grave with the wicked, and with the rich in his death, though he had done no violence" (Isaiah 53:9). Jesus' immediate family didn't have the financial resources to provide Him with a stately burial. But God moved the heart of a wealthy man, and Isaiah's prophecy became a reality when Joseph of Arimathea gifted his own burial site to Jesus (Matthew 27:60). Joseph and Nicodemus were risking the wrath of the Sanhedrin in showing their allegiance to Jesus. At this point, no one was expecting Jesus to rise from the dead. These men were Christ-followers, and they were demonstrating their love.

Father, I give thanks to You that in Your perfect plan, the Son of God transitioned from the humiliation of the cross to being exalted in glory. I pray my life will be a living demonstration of the glory of Christ.

What are you willing to risk for Jesus? Practically speaking, what does it look like for you to show your love for Christ?

The Resurrection

They still did not understand from the Scripture that Jesus had to rise from the dead.

—*John 20:9*

T he death of a loved one is a crushing blow. It must've been a tortuously long weekend for Jesus' disciples. They had been with Jesus constantly for three years and now were convinced the life they had known with Christ was over. They'd given up everything to follow Jesus and still didn't understand what was happening (John 20:9). Undoubtedly, they were grieving, confused, scared for their own safety, and wondering what to do next.

Early on Sunday morning, while it was still dark, Mary Magdalene went to Jesus' tomb and saw the stone had been removed. She panicked because she assumed someone had stolen Jesus' body. Grave robbing was common, and thieves especially liked to rob the graves of wealthy people in the hopes of finding valuables.[29] So Mary Magdalene ran to Peter and John and said, "They have taken the Lord out of the tomb, and we don't know where they have put him!" (v. 2). Peter and John investigated the tomb, and what they found was odd. The tomb was empty, but Jesus' graveclothes were still there, and it didn't look as if they'd been disturbed. If robbers had stolen Jesus' body, it's likely they would've taken the body with the graveclothes.

Something interesting happened when the disciples saw the graveclothes. "Finally the other disciple, who had reached the tomb first, also went inside. He saw and believed" (v. 8). Most theologians agree the disciple being referred to is the apostle John and the author of the gospel by his name. After an excruciating weekend of wondering, waiting, and bewilderment, the stage was set for the greatest news in the history of humanity. What had seemed like the worst event that could transpire would give way to the best news the world has ever received. John had good reason to hope and would soon see the evidence of his belief.

Father, I pray that You will increase my faith. I pray that You will empower me to believe before I have visual evidence. Help me know without a doubt that Your Word is true and that You are a God who keeps His promises.

What event or set of circumstances caused you to believe Jesus is who He said He is? Do you ever ask God to increase your faith? How would you describe faith to a new believer or someone seeking the truth?

Jesus Appears to Mary Magdalene

Mary Magdalene went to the disciples with the news: "I have seen the Lord!" And she told them that he had said these things to her.

—*John 20:18*

Read John 20:11–18

A fter Peter and John returned home, Mary stood outside the tomb, weeping (John 20:10–11). At this point, Mary still believed Jesus was dead, and she was distraught that His body was missing. Mary looked into the tomb, and she saw two angels sitting where Jesus' body had been. They inquired why she was crying. "'They have taken my Lord away,' she said, 'and I don't know where they have put him'" (v. 13).

As Mary said this, she saw Jesus standing there but didn't know it was Him. Mary was devastated with grief and was overwhelmed with the fact that Jesus' body was missing. Mary didn't recognize Jesus, and even after He spoke to her, she mistook Him for the gardener and said, "Sir, if you have carried him away, tell me where you have put him, and I will get him" (v. 15). Jesus put an end to her grief with one word. He spoke her name (v. 16). When Mary heard her name from the voice of the risen Lord, she instantly knew that Jesus had been resurrected from the dead.

In John 10, Jesus described Himself as the "good shepherd" (v. 11). He said, "The gatekeeper opens the gate for him, and the sheep listen to his voice. He calls his own sheep by name and leads them out" (v. 3). Later in the passage, Jesus said, "I am the good shepherd. The good shepherd lays down his life for the sheep"

(v. 11). True to His word, Jesus had laid down His life for Mary and all who would believe in His name. And Mary knew her Shepherd's voice. Naturally, Mary reached to embrace Jesus. Jesus said, "Do not hold on to me, for I have not yet ascended to the Father. Go instead to my brothers and tell them, 'I am ascending to my Father and your Father, to my God and your God'" (20:17). Mary did as Jesus instructed, and as a result, she was the first person to share the news of the resurrected Lord.

Father, the news of the resurrected Christ is the best thing that has ever happened to humanity. Jesus, I pray that I will be like Mary and be quick to tell the news of the gospel. Help me discern Your voice among all the others.

Do you feel compelled to share what Jesus has done in your life? Do you recognize His voice when He speaks to you? How would you respond if you were face-to-face with the risen Lord?

Jesus Appears to the Disciples

Again Jesus said, "Peace be with you! As the Father has sent me, I am sending you."
—*John 20:21*

. . . .

J esus' disciples were gathered together and were undoubtedly discussing the confusing events that had taken place. Peter and John had viewed the empty tomb with their own eyes and had heard Mary Magdalene's testimony that the Lord had risen. Still, they were struggling to come to terms with what had transpired. In fear for their lives, they gathered behind locked doors with the hopes that Jewish leaders wouldn't come looking for Jesus' followers.

As the disciples gathered together, Jesus appeared in their presence and said, "Peace be with you!" (John 20:19). He showed them His hands and pierced side as evidence of His identity. "Peace be with you" or "Peace to you" is a common greeting among Jews. Notably, Jesus repeated it twice (vv. 19, 21). The words resonated back to the conversation He'd had with His disciples just before going to the cross. In the Upper Room the night before the crucifixion, Jesus said, "Peace I leave with you; my peace I give you. I do not give to you as the world gives. Do not let your hearts be troubled and do not be afraid" (14:27). Now He had returned, following His death and resurrection. By saying, "Peace to you" and showing the scars on His body, Jesus was communicating that He had done what He said He was going to do, and because of His sacrifice, all who believe could enjoy peace and reconciliation with the Father.[30]

Then Jesus gave His disciples some instructions: "As the Father has sent me, I am sending you" (20:21). This statement is John's account of Jesus issuing the Great Commission (Matthew 28:19–20; Mark 16:15; Luke 24:47). Jesus commanded His disciples to go to all the world and share the good news of the gospel with every nation and ethnicity. Jesus commissioned His followers to act as His representatives and witnesses to a lost world. The Great Commission was not intended for the first disciples alone but includes every Christ-follower who would come after. As Christians, we are called to share the gospel with those who don't know Christ.

Father, the news of the resurrected Christ is life changing. Empower me to be quick to share what I know about Jesus with others. I pray You will burden my heart for those who don't yet know Christ as Lord.

How would you describe your relationship with Jesus to a nonbeliever? How is your life different because you follow Jesus? Do you feel comfortable sharing your faith? What prevents you from doing so?

The Purpose of This Book

But these are written that you may believe that Jesus is the Messiah, the Son of God, and that by believing you may have life in his name.
—*John 20:31*

Read John 20:30-31

In modern times, it's not uncommon for an author to include his or her thesis at the beginning of a book. A good thesis provides the reader with the reason the author is writing. The apostle John saved his thesis for the end of his gospel. John shared that the reason he provided a written account of the life and ministry of Christ was so readers would believe Jesus is the Messiah and the Son of God (John 20:31). But John didn't limit his goal of writing merely so the reader would believe facts about Christ that proved His identity. John wrote with the intention that the reader would believe and as a result "have life in his name" (v. 31).

Scores of people believe in Jesus' existence but don't serve Him as Lord. The apostle James wrote, "You believe that there is one God. Good! Even the demons believe that—and shudder" (James 2:19). James's point was that it's possible to believe in Christ's existence and not possess saving faith. So the apostle John's goal in writing his gospel was to prove that Jesus was who He said He was and for the reader to not only believe but also experience life in His name (John 20:31). Jesus said, "I have come that they may have life, and have it to the full" (10:10). It's possible to know a lot of facts and information about Jesus without knowing Jesus. The apostle

John urged his readers to possess knowledge about Christ and a saving relationship that produces both abundant and eternal life.

If we believe that Jesus is the Son of God who died on the cross for our sins and was resurrected on the third day, we can experience life in His name. But Jesus says those who love Him will obey His Word and by doing so will serve Him as Lord (14:15). The apostle Paul wrote, "For if, while we were God's enemies, we were reconciled to him through the death of his Son, how much more, having been reconciled, shall we be saved through his life!" (Romans 5:10).

Jesus, I ask for the kind of relationship with You that can only be described as the greatest joy of my life. I pray that I will know You well and be obedient to Your Word and Your calling on my life. I pray that I will live my life in a manner that proclaims Your glory.

How would you describe the difference between knowing a lot of information about Jesus and knowing Him as Lord? How would you describe your relationship with Christ? What steps can you take to know Jesus in a deeper way?

Jesus and the Beloved Apostle

Jesus did many other things as well. If every one of them were written down, I suppose that even the whole world would not have room for the books that would be written.

—*John 21:25*

J ohn concluded his gospel by answering a few questions that bring closure to his account of the life of Christ. Jesus had ended His conversation with Peter by saying, "Follow me!" (John 21:19). Following Christ is a nonnegotiable of the Christian life. Earlier in John's gospel, Jesus said, "Whoever serves me must follow me; and where I am, my servant also will be. My Father will honor the one who serves me" (12:26). Jesus and Peter had been in a deep discussion, and Jesus had predicted that Peter would die as a martyr for Christ (21:18–19). Shortly after, Peter saw the apostle John. "When Peter saw him, he asked, 'Lord, what about him?'" (v. 21).

Peter's question was likely prompted by Jesus' statement about Peter's coming martyrdom. Jesus mildly rebuked Peter and said, "If I want him to remain alive until I return, what is that to you? You must follow me" (v. 22). Jesus wasn't indicating that John would live until His return; He was telling Peter to tend to his own business and be mindful of his own devotion to Christ.[31] Jesus' statement sparked a rumor that John would stay alive until Christ's return, but John was quick to let his readers know that wasn't what Jesus had said. Church history teaches that John is the only one of the disciples who didn't die as a martyr for the faith, but he did experience persecution when he was exiled to the island of Patmos, and it was there that he wrote the book of Revelation.

John closed his gospel by reminding his audience that everything he wrote was true, but it wasn't exhaustive. John was an eyewitness to the life and ministry of Jesus Christ, but it was impossible to record everything the Son of God did during His earthly ministry. John believed it was necessary to attest to his own credibility by taking an oath at the end of his gospel (v. 24). As a Jew, John understood the importance of an oath and the punishment for false witness.[32] So, at the conclusion of his gospel, he took an oath and wrote, "We know that his testimony is true" (v. 24).

Father, I thank You that You have provided a written account of Your Word. I am grateful that because of the Scriptures, I can know Jesus. I pray that the truths I read in Your Word will be living and active in me and that I will live my life as a Christ-follower who loves Jesus and obeys the Scriptures.

Do you believe that the apostle John's account of the life and ministry of Christ is true? If so, how does it impact your relationship with Christ?

Notes

1. D. A. Carson, *The Farewell Discourse and Final Prayer of Jesus: An Exposition of John 14–17* (Grand Rapids: Baker Book House, 1980), 9.
2. John MacArthur, *The MacArthur New Testament Commentary: John 1–11* (Chicago: Moody, 2006), 1–2.
3. D. A. Carson, *The Gospel According to John*, Pillar New Testament Commentary (Grand Rapids: William B. Eerdmans, 1991), 115–18.
4. MacArthur, *The MacArthur New Testament Commentary: John 1–11*, 77–82.
5. R. C. Sproul, *John*: St. Andrew's Expositional Commentary (Sanford: Ligonier Ministries, 2009), 20.
6. MacArthur, *The MacArthur New Testament Commentary: John 1–11*, 89–91.
7. MacArthur, 103–4.
8. Carson, *The Gospel According to John*, 243.
9. MacArthur, *The MacArthur New Testament Commentary: John 1–11*, 176.
10. Sproul, *John*, 122.
11. MacArthur, *The MacArthur New Testament Commentary: John 1–11*, 300.
12. MacArthur, 427–29.
13. Sproul, *John*, 205.
14. MacArthur, 466–67.
15. MacArthur, 472–75.
16. Leon Morris, *The Gospel According to John*: The New International Commentary of the New Testament, (Grand Rapids: Eerdmans, 1995), 499.
17. Sproul, *John*, 218.
18. John MacArthur, *The MacArthur New Testament Commentary: John 12–21* (Chicago: Moody, 2006), 9–10.
19. MacArthur, 38.
20. Sproul, *John*, 271.
21. Sproul, 271.
22. MacArthur, *The MacArthur New Testament Commentary: John 12–21*, 195.
23. Sproul, *John*, 337.
24. MacArthur, *The MacArthur New Testament Commentary: John 12–21*, 320–21.
25. MacArthur, 326–27.
26. MacArthur, 337–38.
27. MacArthur, 352–53.
28. Sproul, *John*, 374–76.
29. Sproul, 383–84.
30. Sproul, 390.
31. MacArthur, *The MacArthur New Testament Commentary: John 12–21*, 404–5.
32. Sproul, *John*, 407–8.